Water

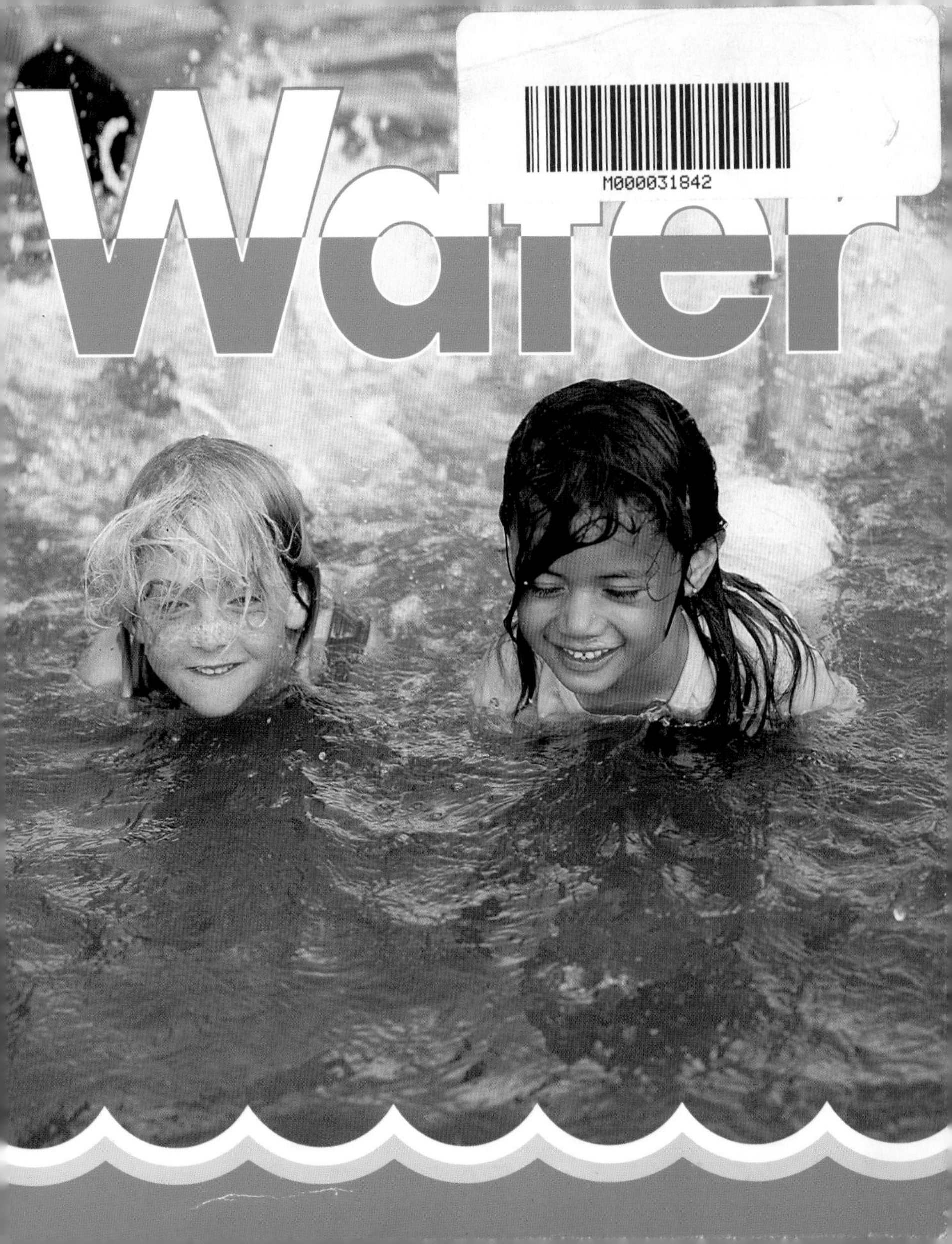

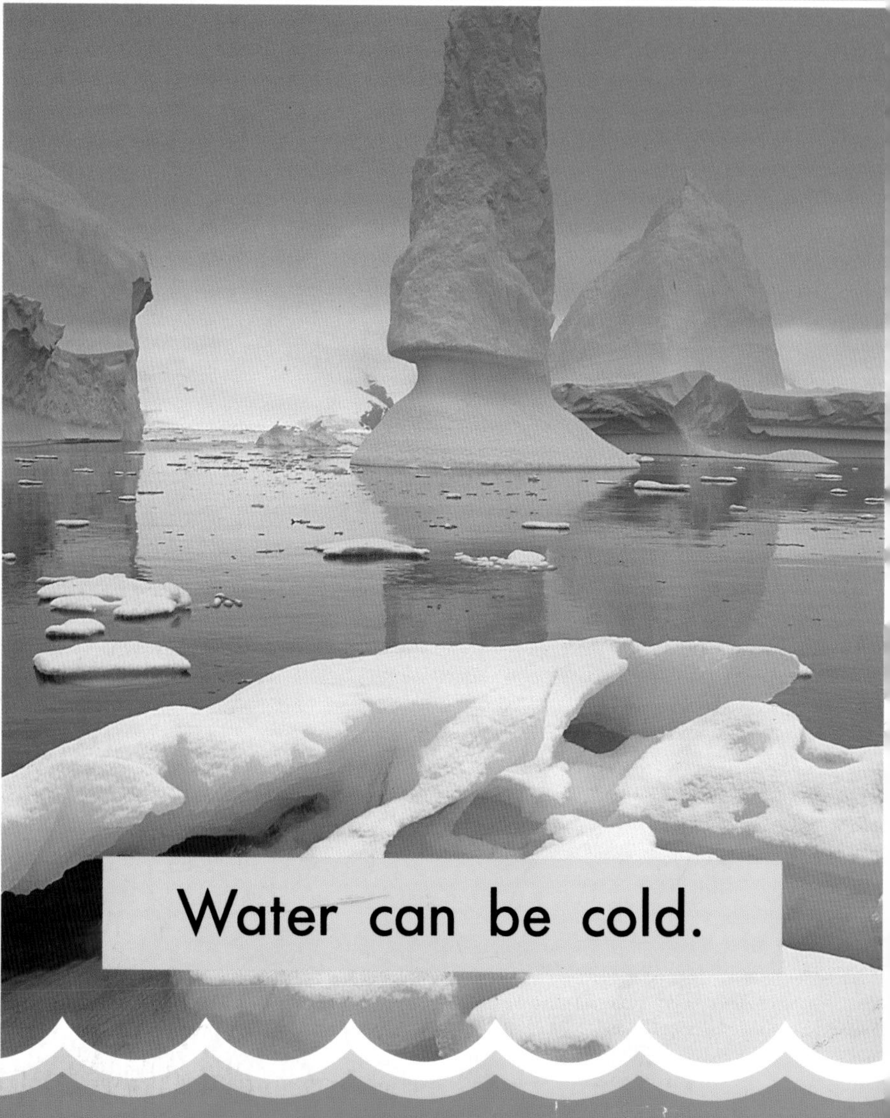

Water can be cold.

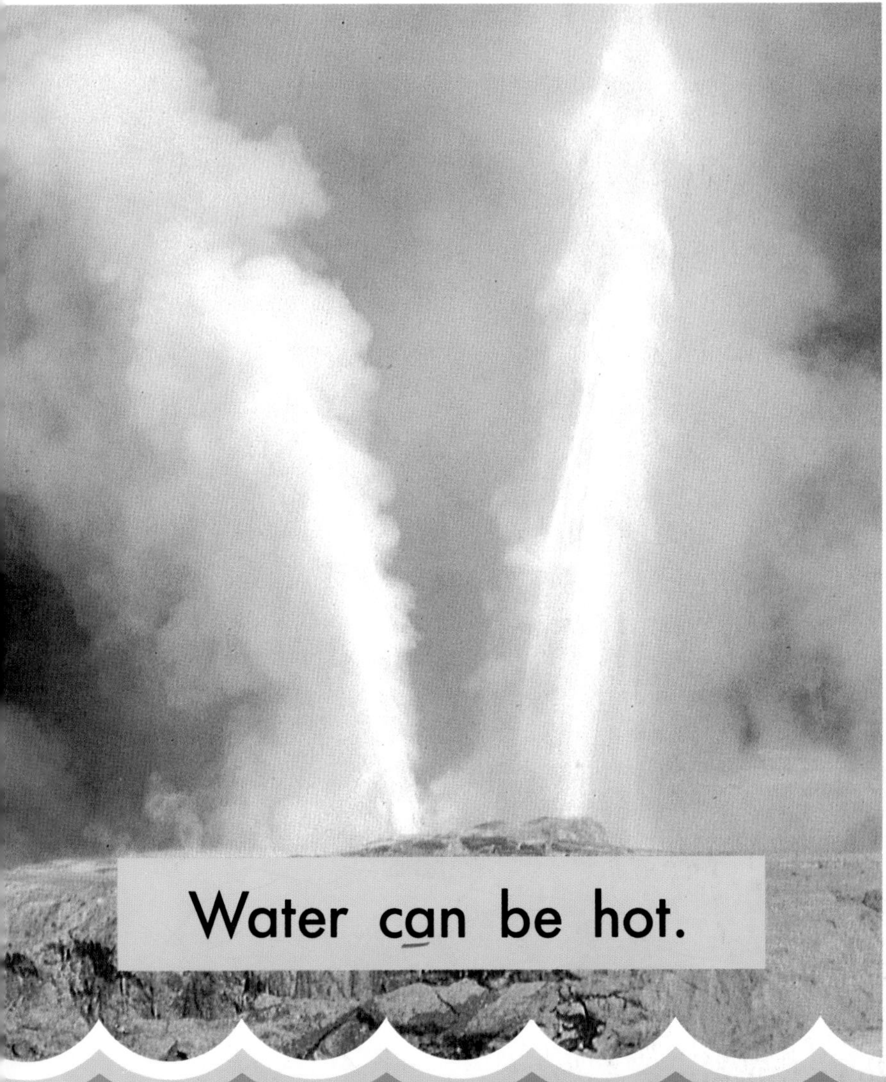

Water can be hot.

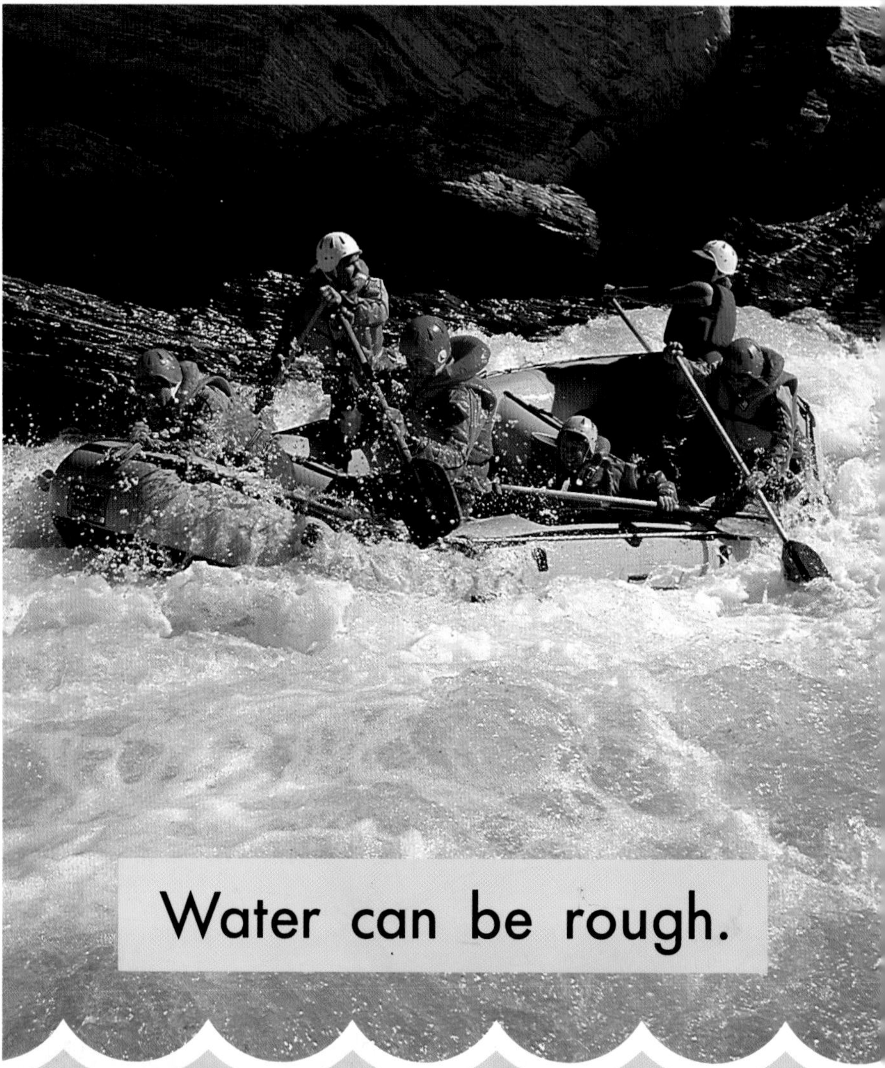

Water can be rough.

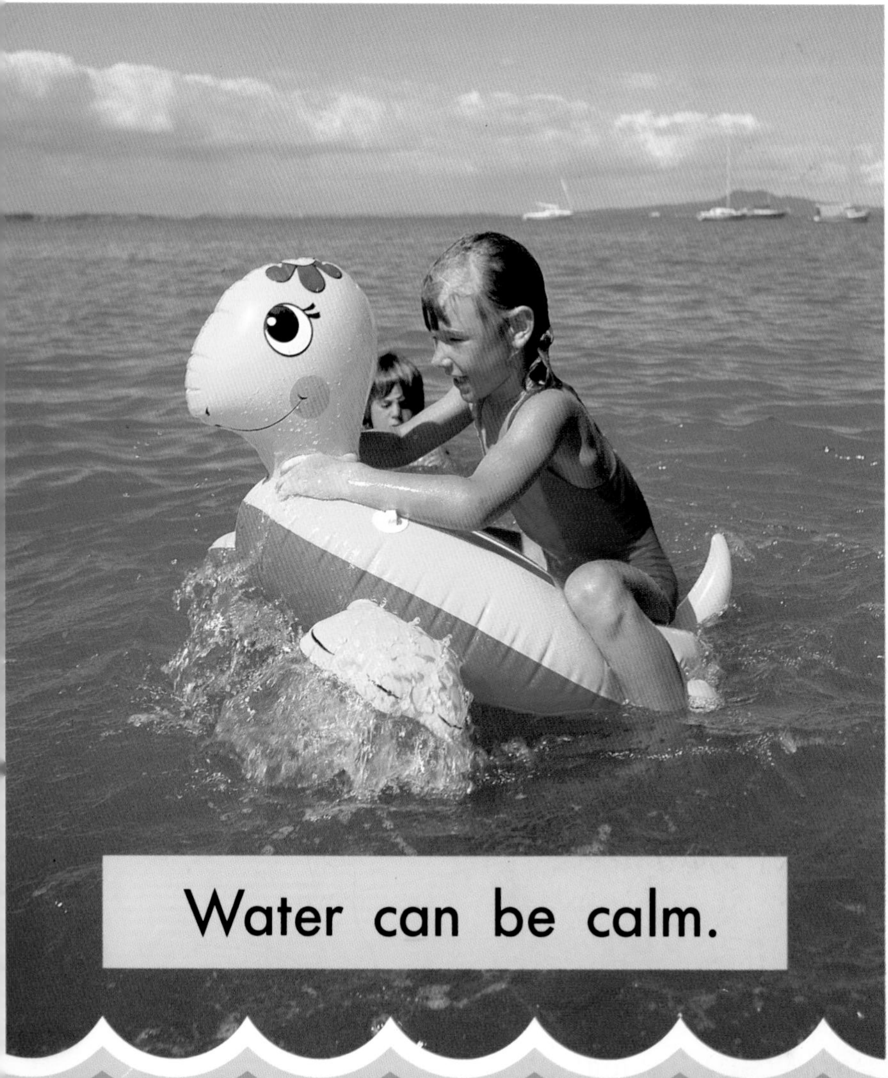

Water can be calm.

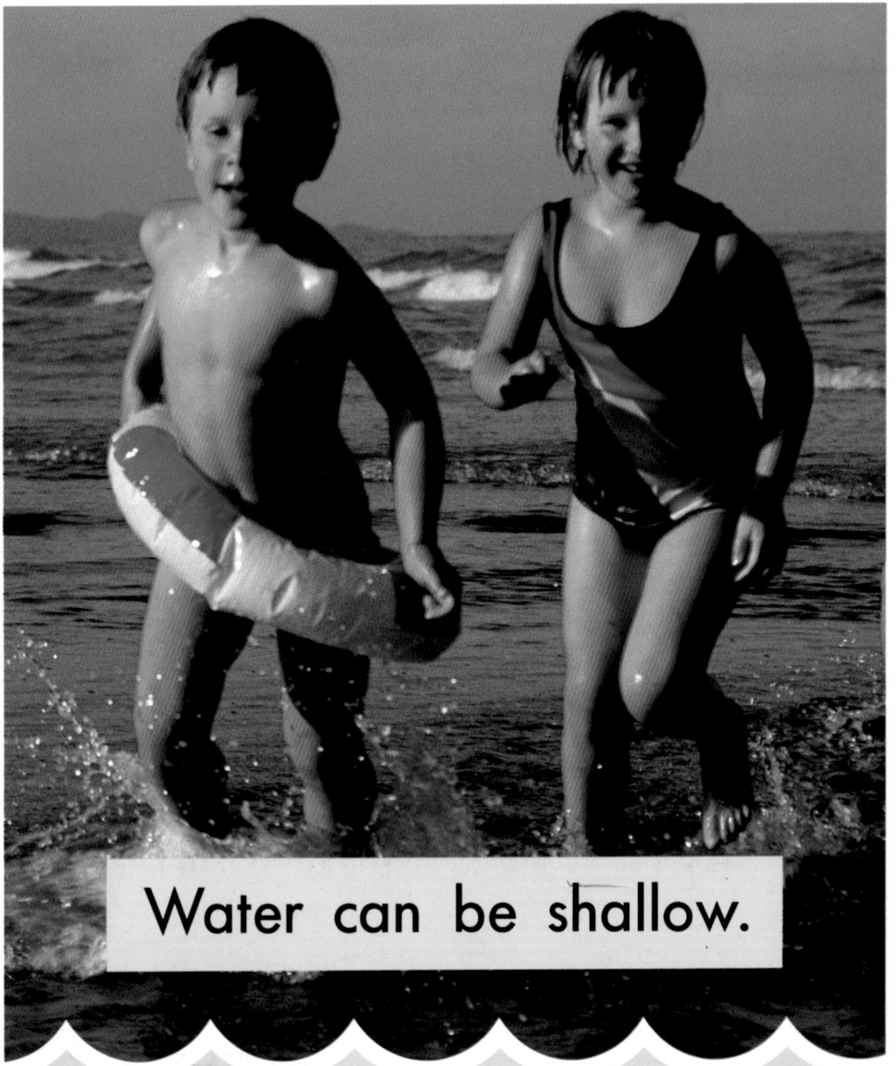

Water can be shallow.

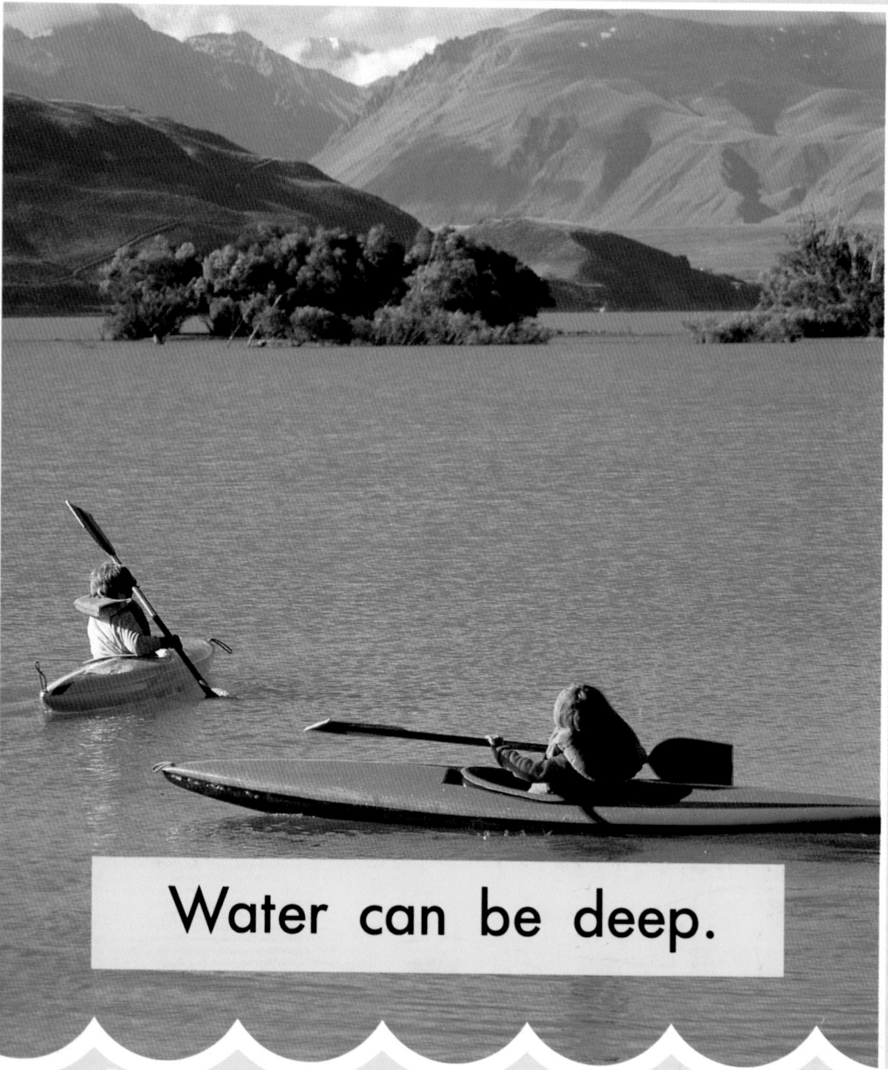

Water can be deep.

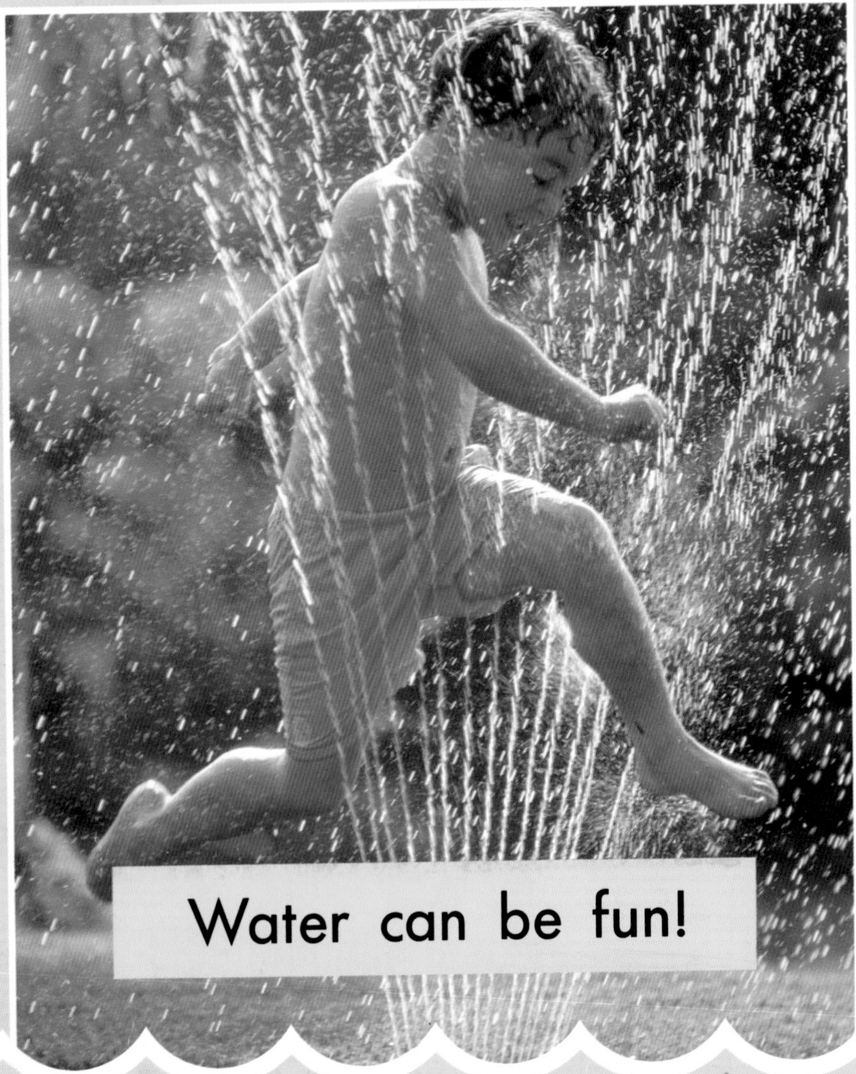

Water can be fun!